D0241878

ANIMAL COLOURS

QED Publishing

fish

shrimp

mite

bird

RED

salamander

ladybird

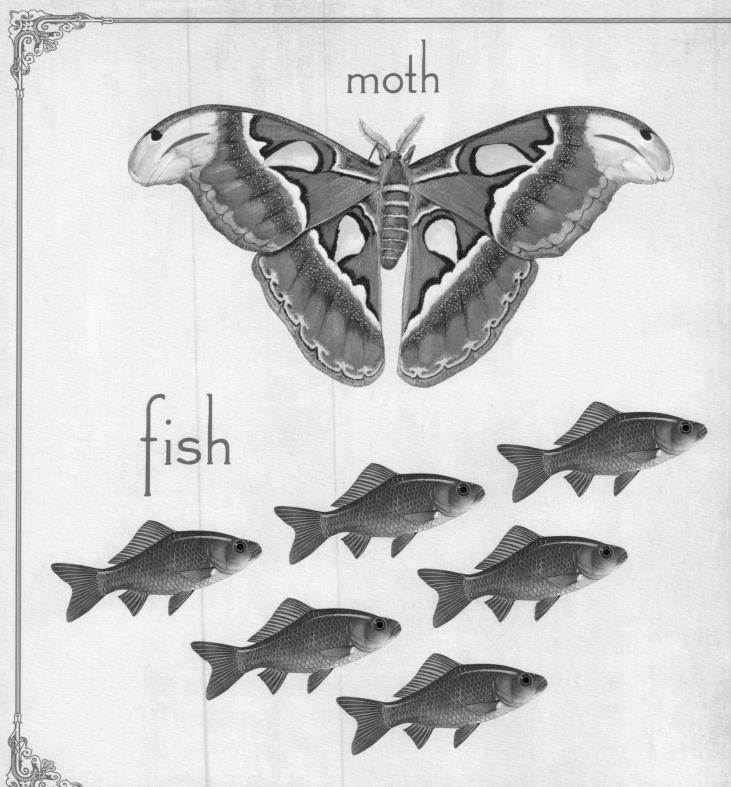

moth

fish

newt

beetle

ORANGE

starfish

shell

scorpion

frog

YELLOW

fish

octopus

bird

caterpillar

butterfly

spider

frog

birds

chameleon

snake

frog

GREEN

BLUE

damselfly

bird

lizard

butterfly

bird

fish

bird

PURPLE

bird

jellyfish

ray

BLACK

beetle

slug

spider

frog

gorilla

WHITE

whale

rabbit

swan

polar
bear

oryx

bird

fox

GREY

hippopotamus

cuckoo

possum

dolphin

flamingo

fish

PINK

squid

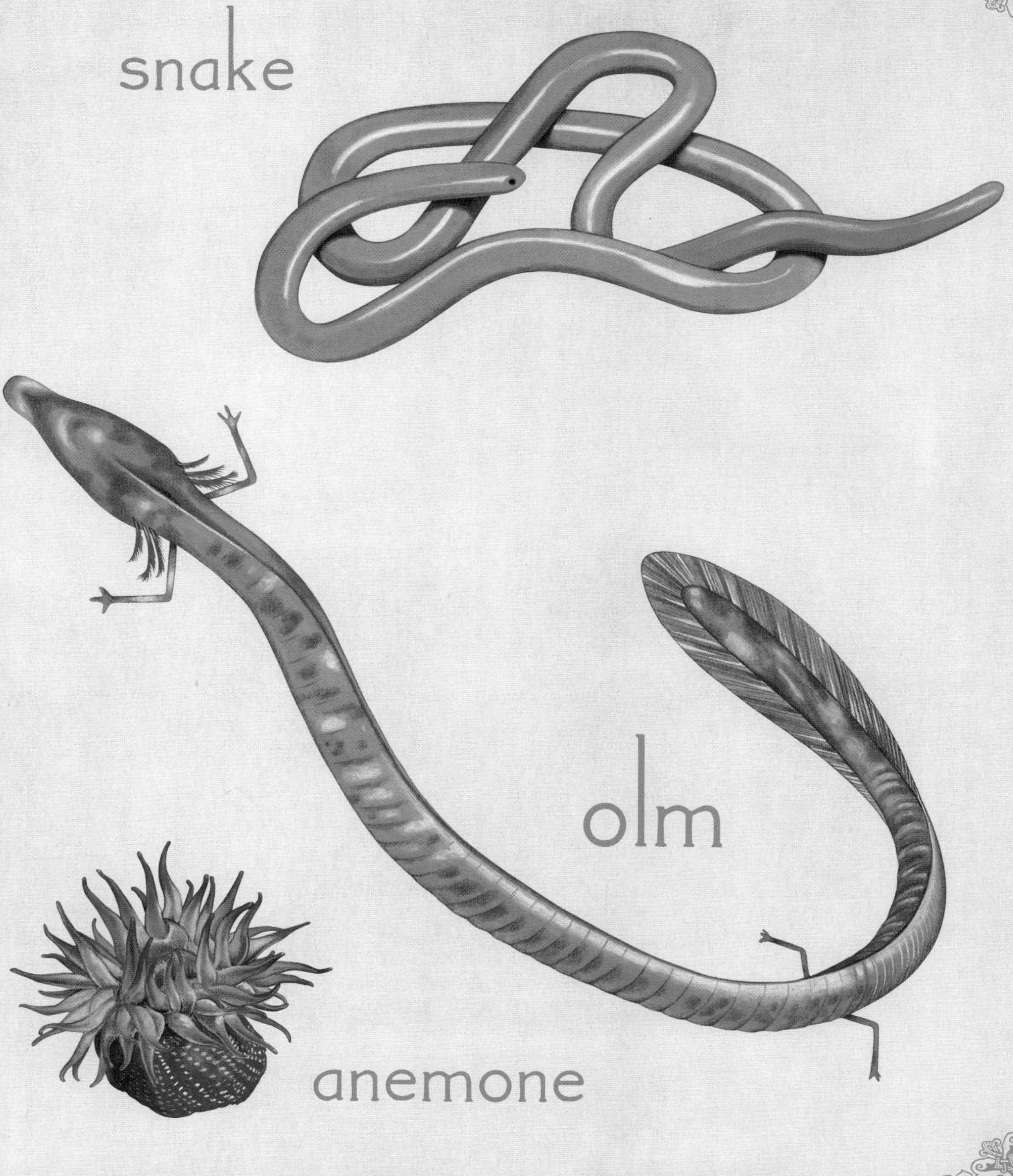

PINK PINK PINK PINK PINK PINK PINK PINK PINK

snake

olm

anemone

PINK PINK PINK PINK PINK PINK PINK PINK PINK

sawfish

beaver

lizard

bird

eagle

groundhog

kiwi

moose

walrus

bear

BROWN

fish

SILVER

lion

GOLD

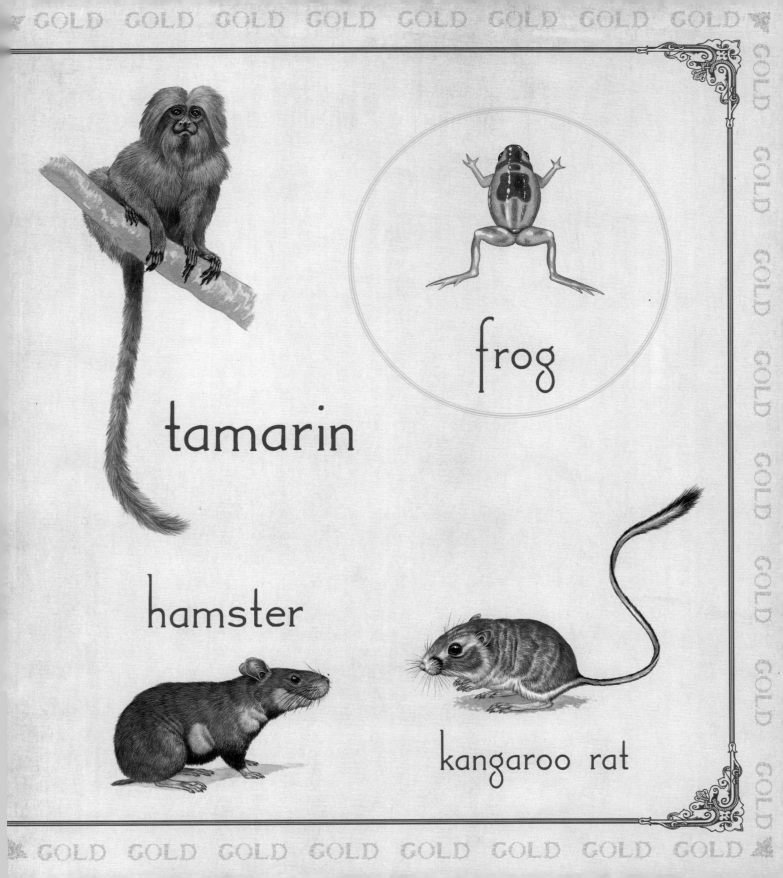

tamarin

frog

hamster

kangaroo rat

red

orange

yellow   green   blue

RAINBOW COLOURS

indigo   violet

QUIZ

How many green
animals can you find?

What colour is
the flamingo?

Is a kangaroo
rat purple?

Is the slug blue?

What colour is
the possum?

What colours
can you see
on this parrot?

Is the
moth green?

QED Publishing, a Quarto Group company
The Old Brewery
6 Blundell Street
London N7 9BH

www.ced_publishing.co.uk

A catalogue record for this book is available from the British Library.

ISBN 978 1 78171 684 7

Printed and bound in China by
1010 Printing International Ltd